2015 GREATEST
ROCK & POP HITS
21 Current Hits

for PIANO

Produced by
Alfred Music
P.O. Box 10003
Van Nuys, CA 91410-0003
alfred.com

Printed in USA.

ISBN-10: 1-4706-2007-3
ISBN-13: 978-1-4706-2007-3

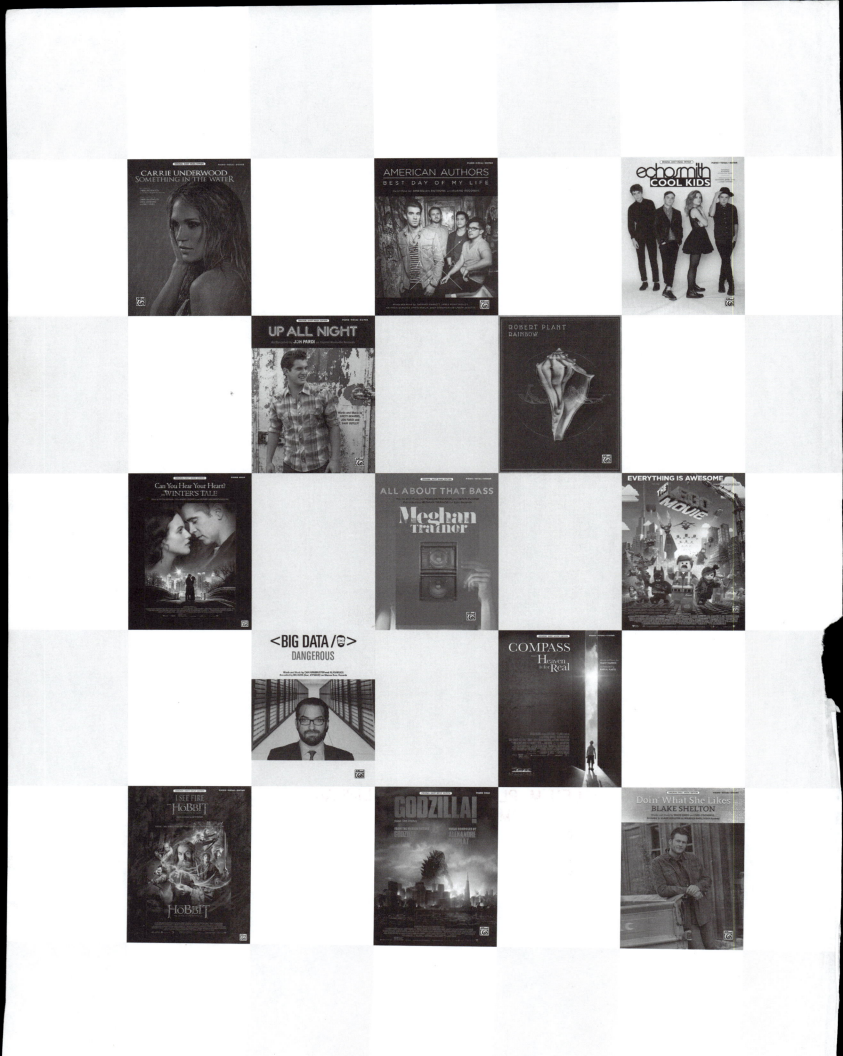

CONTENTS

ALL ABOUT THAT BASS

Words and Music by
MEGHAN TRAINOR and KEVIN KADISH

Verse 1:

1. Yeah, it's pret - ty clear, I ain't no size two,___ but I can shake it, shake it like I'm sup-posed to do. 'Cause I got that boom, boom_ that all the boys chase. And all___ the right junk_ in all___ the right plac - es. I see a mag - a - zine work-ing that Pho - to - shop._ We know that shit ain't_ real, come on now, make it stop.

8

Verse 2:

Chorus:

bass.   Be - cause you know I'm   bass.

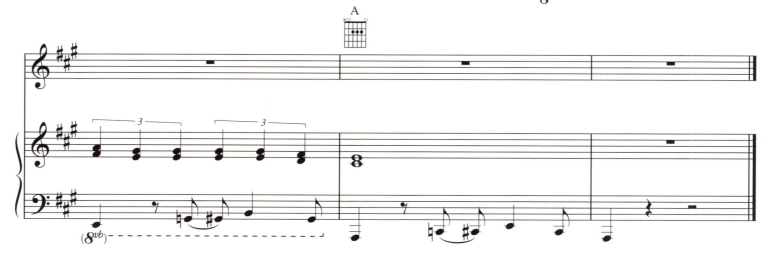

ALONE YET NOT ALONE

Lyric by
DENNIS SPIEGEL

Music by
BRUCE BROUGHTON

14

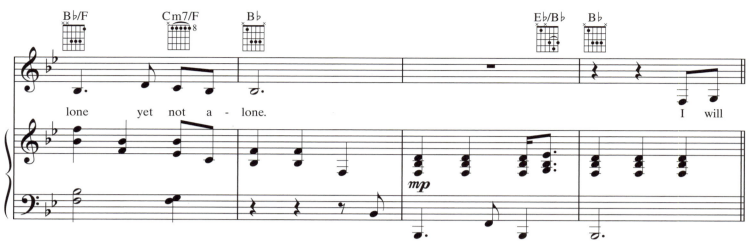

lone yet not a - lone.   I will

not   be bent in   fear.   He's the ref - uge I know is near.   In His

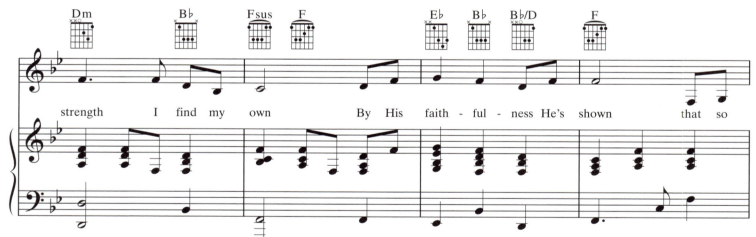

strength   I find my   own   By His faith - ful - ness He's shown   that so

might - y is His shield.   All His love   is now re - vealed.

stum - ble, or I'm thrown, I'm a - lone yet not a - lone.

When my steps are lost and des-p'rate for a guide,

I can feel His touch, a sooth-ing pres - ence by my side, by my

side._____ He has armed_ me___ with His

cresc. poco a poco

love._____ Watch-ful an - gels look from a - bove. Ev - 'ry e - vil can be

braved for I know I will be saved. Nev - er fright - ened on my

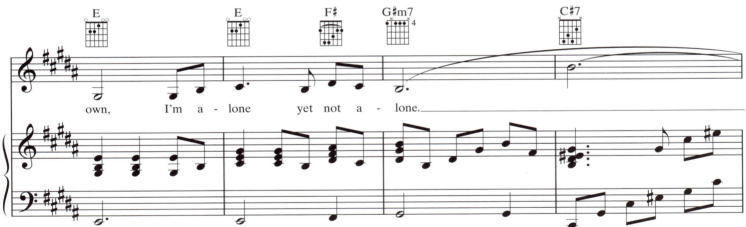

own, I'm a - lone yet not a - lone._____

Freely

_____ I'm a - lone yet not a - lone._____

BEST DAY OF MY LIFE

Words and Music by
ZACHARY BARNETT, JAMES ADAM SHELLEY,
MATTHEW SANCHEZ, DAVID RUBLIN,
SHEP GOODMAN and AARON ACCETTA

Moderate rock ♩ = 96

Best Day of My Life - 7 - 1

woo. Woo, woo,_____ woo. 2. I

Verse 2:

N.C.

howl - ed at the moon with friends,____ and then the sun came crash - ing in._____

Whoa-oh - oh - oh - oh - oh-oh.____
(Whoa-oh - oh - oh - oh-oh-oh.)____ But all the poss - i - bil - i - ties,____ no

lim - its, just e - piph - an - ies.____ Whoa-oh - oh - oh - oh - oh-oh.____
(Whoa-oh - oh - oh - oh - oh-oh.)____ I'm

Chorus:

22

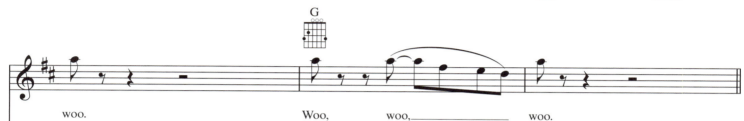

Bridge:

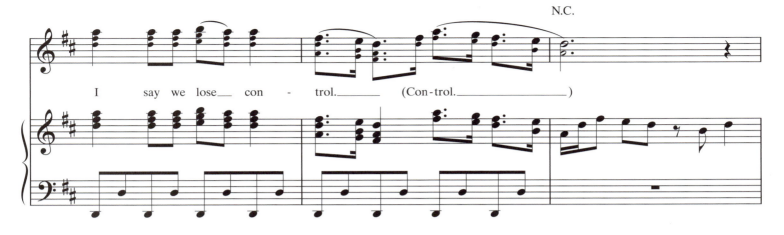

I say we lose___ con - trol._____ (Con - trol._____)

Woo,   woo,_____   woo.

Chorus:

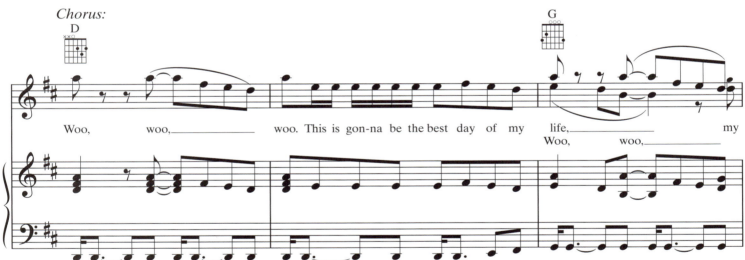

Woo,   woo,_____   woo. This is gon-na be the best day of my   life,_____   my
Woo,   woo,_____

li - i - i - i - i - i -ife.____ Woo,   woo,_____   woo. This is gon-na be the best day of my
woo.

CAN YOU HEAR YOUR HEART?

(from *Winter's Tale*)

Music by
HANS ZIMMER, ANN MARIE CALHOUN
and RUPERT GREGSON-WILLIAMS

Slowly and tenderly (♩ = 73)

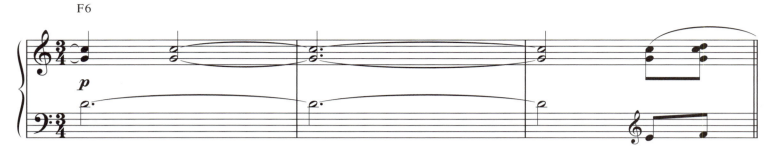

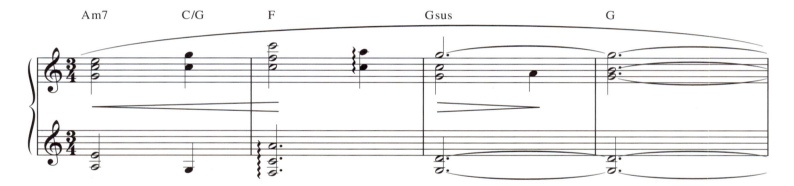

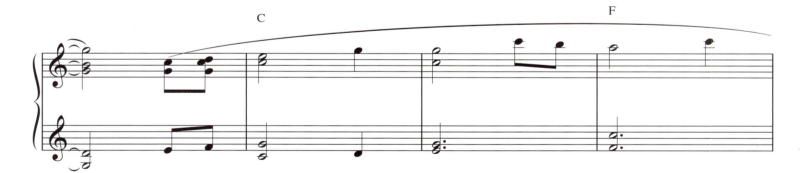

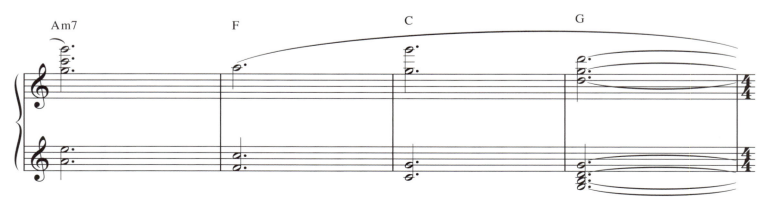

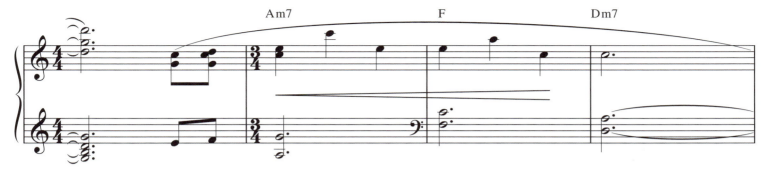

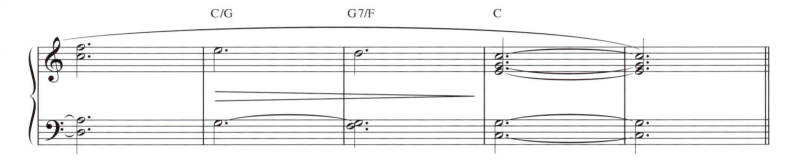

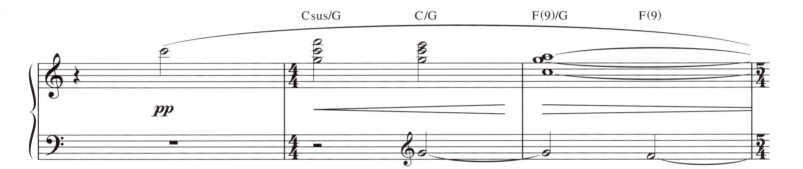

28

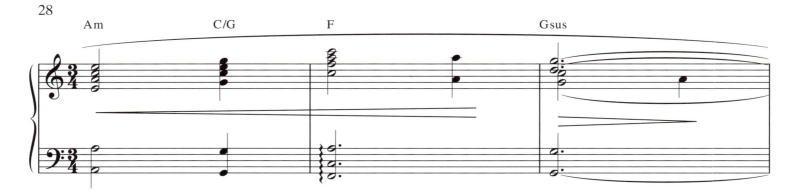

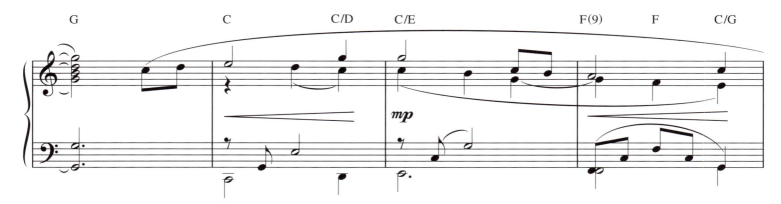

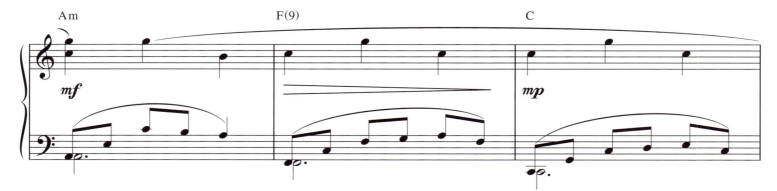

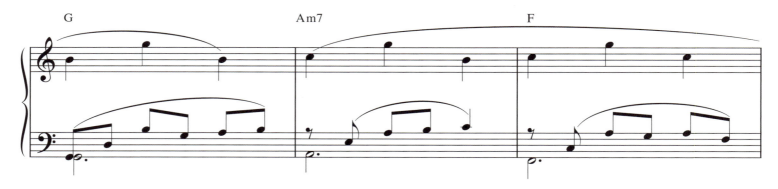

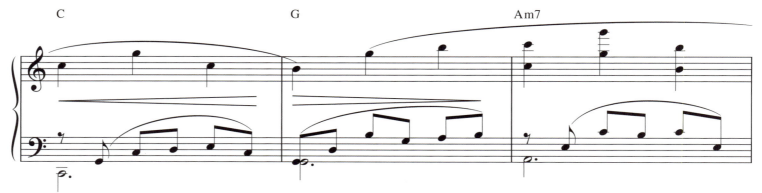

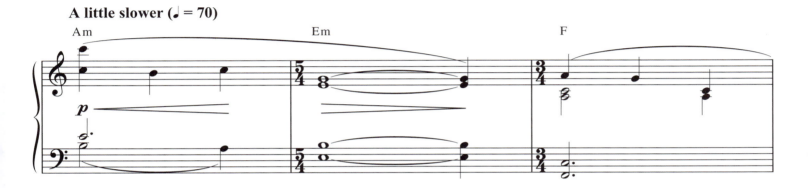

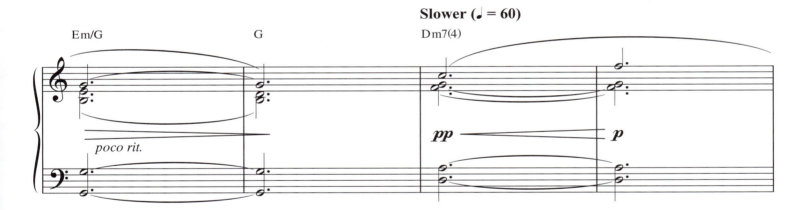

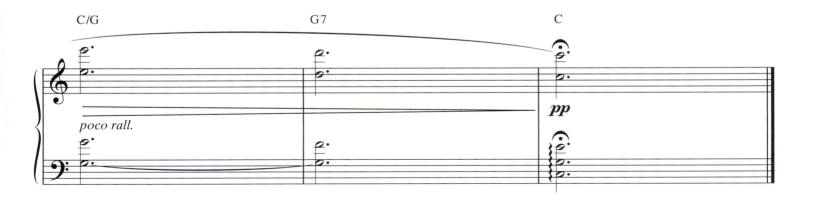

CLOUDS

Words and Music by
ZACH SOBIECH

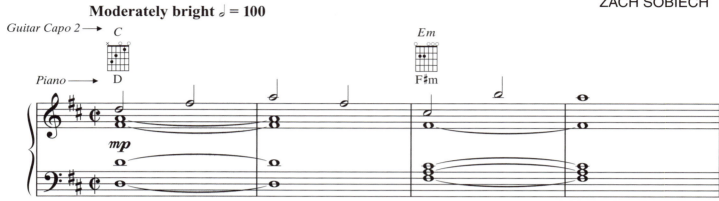

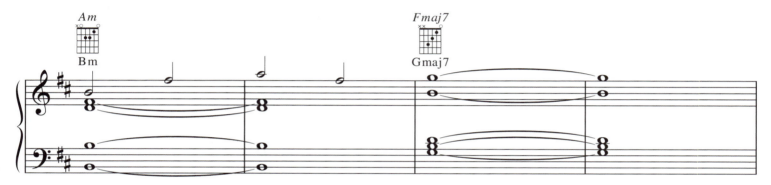

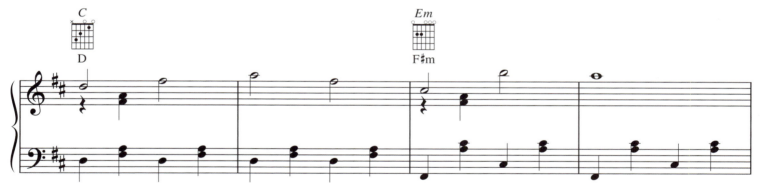

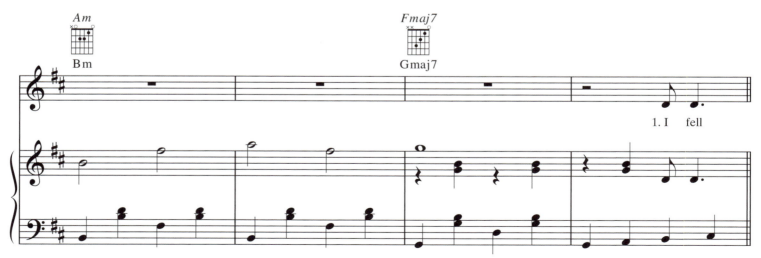

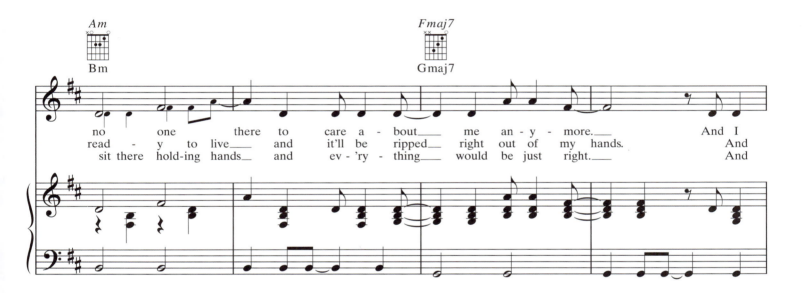

34

with   you._____ 3. We   could___ go

＋ *Coda*

_____ now._____

rall.

molto rit.

COMING UP ROSES

(from *Begin Again*)

Words and Music by
GLEN HANSARD and
DANIELLE BRISEBOIS

*Original recording in B♭m, guitar capo 1.

Coming Up Roses - 7 - 1

some-thing's got-ta change.___

but it's me who's got to change.___

Chorus:

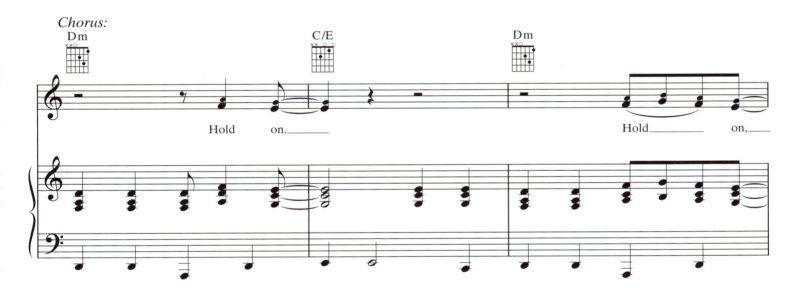

Hold on.___   Hold___ on,___

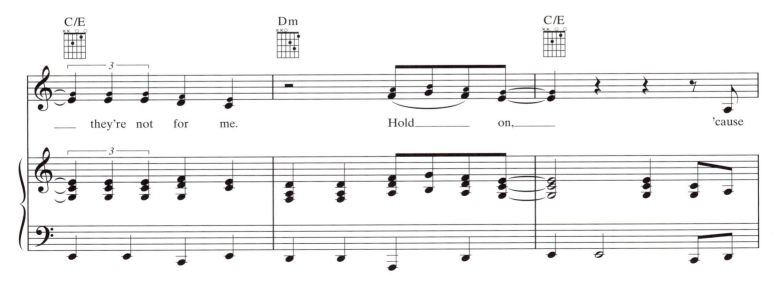

___ they're not for me.   Hold___ on,___   'cause

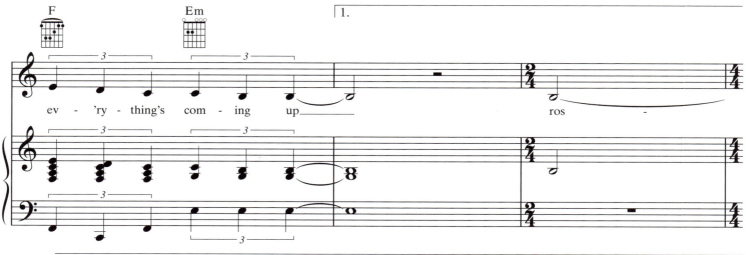

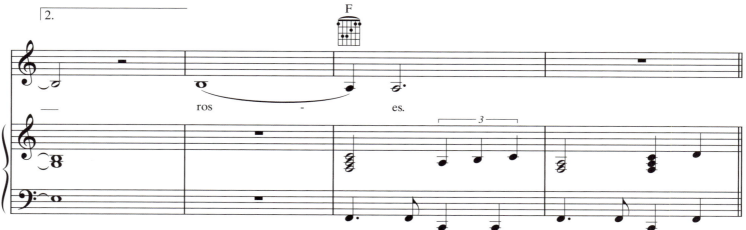

COMPASS

Words and Music by
DIANE WARREN

Verse 1 (sing 1st time only):

1. When night___ is fall - ing so hard_ up-on___ you,___

Verse 2 (sing 2nd time only):

2. When night___ has paint - ed your world_ in shad - ows,___

and the world is hang - ing___ heav - y on_____ your heart,_

and you're left feel - ing left out in_____ the cold,_

*Play chord 1st time only.

44

Chorus:

and think no one__ can find__ you, I will__ re - mind__ you you're not__ a - lone. I will be there,__ I'll be the one__ to guide__ you. My love will be your com - pass. I will lead_____ you home.

Chorus:

and think no one__ can find__ you,____ I____ will re - mind_

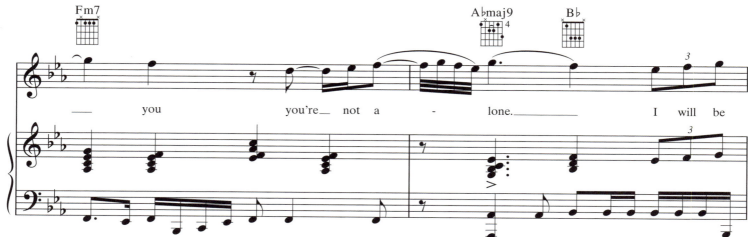

__ you you're__ not a - lone._____ I will be

there, I'll be the one_____ to guide__ you.____ My love will be your

com - pass._____ I will lead you home._____

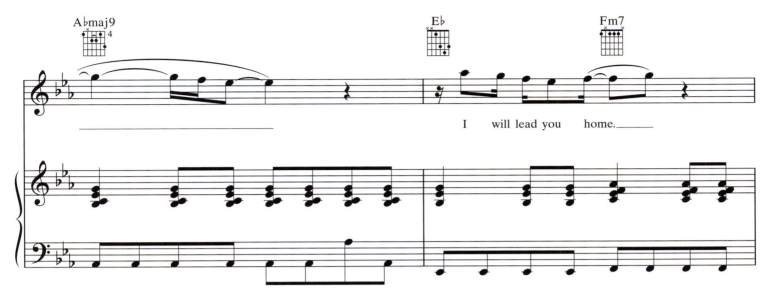

I will lead you home.___

Let my love___ be your com - pass. I will lead you

home._____ I will lead you home.

molto rit. e dim.

COOL KIDS

Words and Music by
GRAHAM SIEROTA, JAMIE SIEROTA,
NOAH SIEROTA, SYDNEY SIEROTA,
JEFFERY DAVID SIEROTA and JESIAH DZWONEK

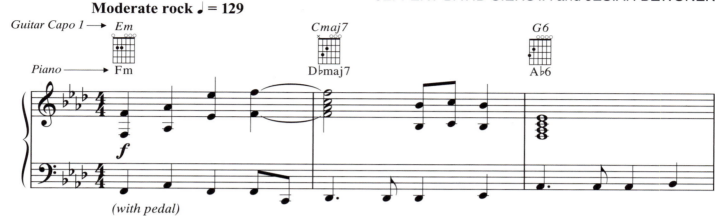

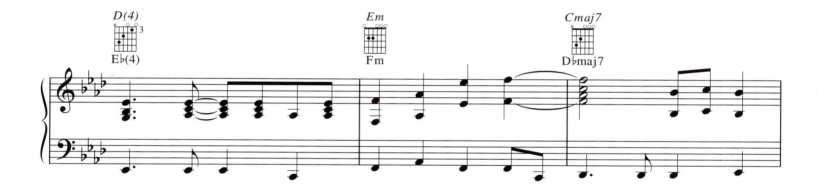

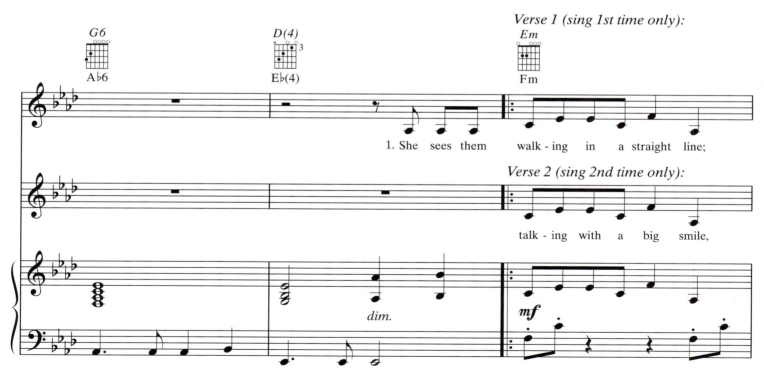

1. She sees them walk-ing in a straight line;

Verse 2 (sing 2nd time only):

talk-ing with a big smile,

be like the cool kids, like the cool kids." _____

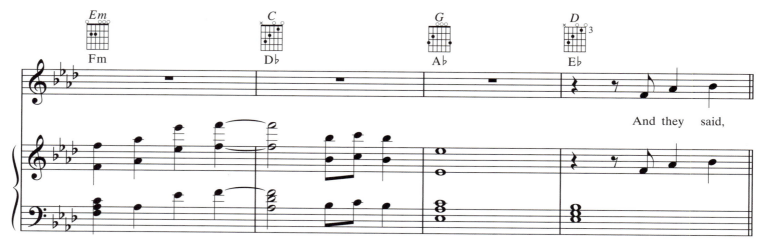

And they said,

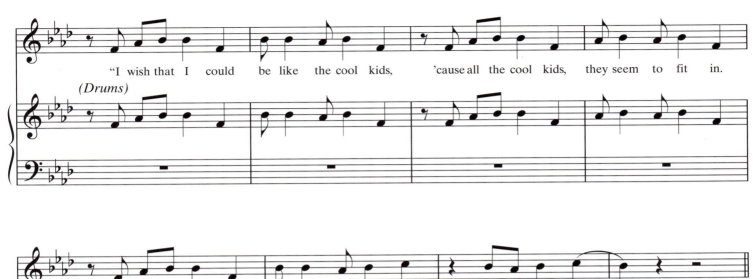

"I wish that I could be like the cool kids, 'cause all the cool kids, they seem to fit in.
(Drums)

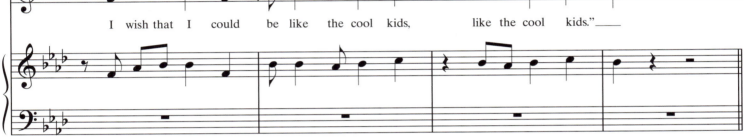

I wish that I could be like the cool kids, like the cool kids."____

Chorus:

"I wish that I could be like the cool kids, 'cause all the cool kids, they seem to fit in.

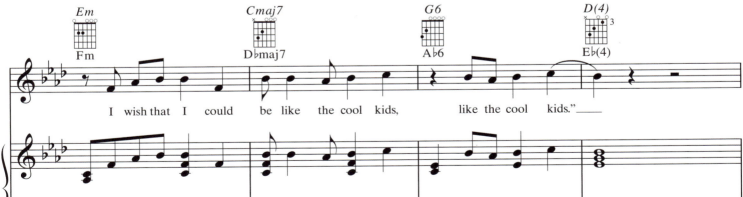

I wish that I could be like the cool kids, like the cool kids."____

54

"I wish that I could be like the cool kids, 'cause all the cool kids, they seem to get it.

I wish that I could be like the cool kids, like the cool kids."____

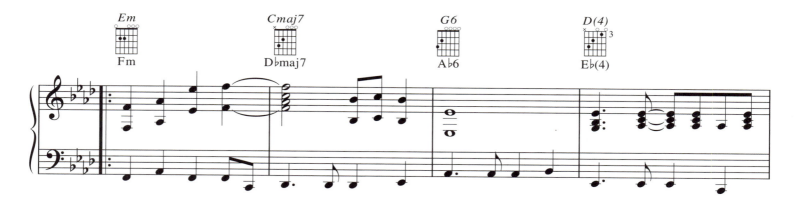

Repeat ad lib. and fade

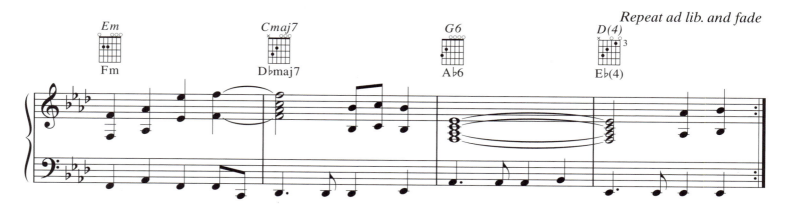

EVERYTHING IS AWESOME
(Awesome Remixxx!!!)

Lyrics by
SHAWN PATTERSON, ANDY SAMBERG,
AKIVA SCHAFFER, JORMA TACCONE,
JOSHUA BARTHOLOMEW and LISA HARRITON

Music by
SHAWN PATTERSON

Ev-'ry-thing is awe-some.___ Ev-'ry-thing is cool when you're part of a team___ Ev-'ry-thing is awe-some___ when we're liv-ing our___ dream.

Everything Is Awesome - 11 - 1

56 *Bridge:*

Ev - 'ry-thing is bet - ter when we stick to - geth - er.

Side by side, you and I gon - na win for - ev -

er. Let's par - ty for - ev - er.

We're the same, I'm like you, you're like me. We're all work -

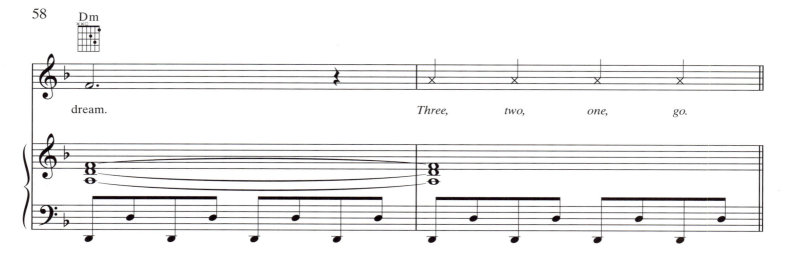

dream.

Three, *two,* *one,* *go.*

Rap 1:

N.C.

Rap 1: See additional lyrics

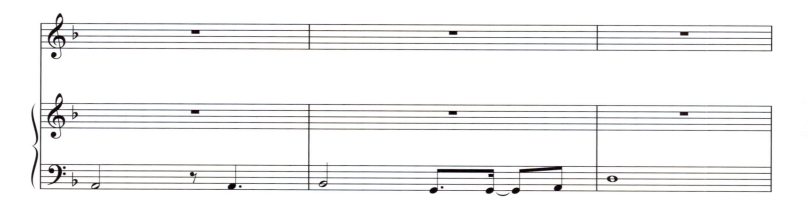

Rap 2:
See additional lyrics

Rap 2: See additional lyrics

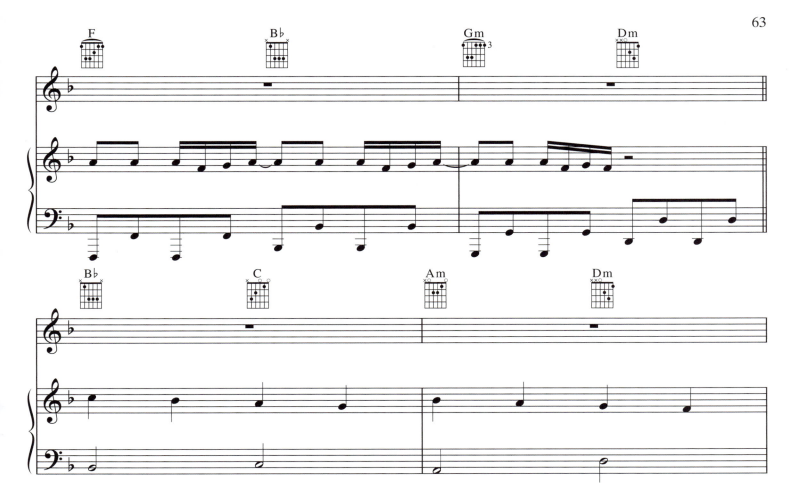

N.C.

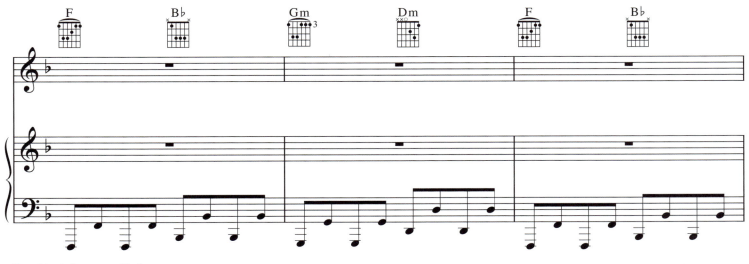

64

Everything Is Awesome - 11 - 10

cool when you're part of a team.___ Ev-'ry-thing is awe-some___

when we're liv-ing our___ dream.

Rap 1:

Have you heard the news? Everyone's talkin'.
Life is good cause everything's awesome.
Lost my job, there's a new opportunity,
More free time for my awesome community.
I feel more awesome than an awesome possum,
Dip my body in chocolate frostin'.
Three years later wash off the frostin'.
Smellin' like a blossom, everything is awesome.
Stepped in mud, got new brown shoes.
It's awesome to win and it's awesome to lose.
(To Bridge:)

Rap 2:

Blue skies, bouncy springs,
We just named two awesome things.
A Nobel Prize, a piece of string.
You know what's awesome? EVERYTHING!
Dogs with fleas,
Allergies,
A book of Greek antiquities,
Brand new pants, a very old vest,
Awesome items are the best.
Trees, frogs, clogs, they're awesome!
Rocks, clocks and socks, they're awesome!
Figs and jigs and twigs, that's awesome!
Everything you see or think or say is awesome!
(To Chorus:)

DANGEROUS

Words and Music by
ALAN WILKIS and DANIEL ARMBRUSTER

out-side and creep-ing to the door, it's like they know. Now they com-ing, yeah,

now they com-ing out from the shad-ows to take me to the club be-cause they

know that I shut this down, 'cause they been watch-ing all my win-dows. They

Chorus:
C

gath-ered up the wall and list-'ning. You un-der-stand, they got a plan for us. I bet

A♭maj7

68

Dangerous - 10 - 4

72

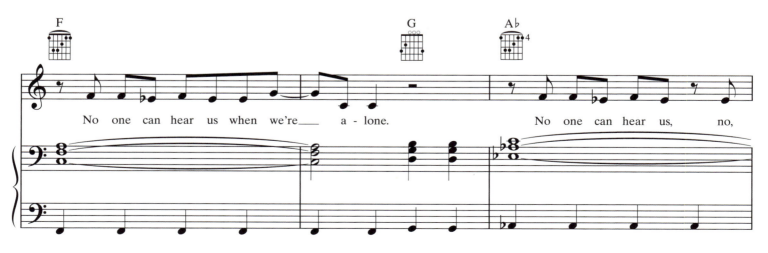

Dangerous - 10 - 7

DOIN' WHAT SHE LIKES

Words and Music by
WADE KIRBY and PHIL O'DONNELL

Verse 1 (sing 1st time only):

____ it when I call in sick to work, ____ spend the whole day hang-ing with her. ____ I

Verse 2 (sing 2nd time only):

____ it when I get past sec-ond gear, sees grav-el fly-ing in the rear-view mirror.

(with pedal)

Doin' What She Likes - 6 - 1

might get fired,_ but that's al - right._ I'm do - in' what_ she likes._ She likes_

Some-times I'm_ push - in' nine-ty-five do - in' what_ she likes._ And she likes_

_ it when I bring home fresh fa - ji - tas and mix up a pitch-er of mar - ga - ri - tas,

_ it when I find a road_that's dark._ Can we pull off_ some - where_ and park? Turn the

78

Like_ run-ning my fin - gers through her long hair, light-in' wa-ter-mel-on can - dles up - stairs,

To Coda ⊕

let - tin' them burn_ and hold - in' her_____ all_____ night._____ I like do - in' what_ she likes._

_____ 2. She likes_

EVERYTHING I DIDN'T SAY

Words and Music by
ASHTON IRWIN, JOHN FELDMANN,
CALUM HOOD and NICHOLAS RAS FURLONG

Everything I Didn't Say - 6 - 1

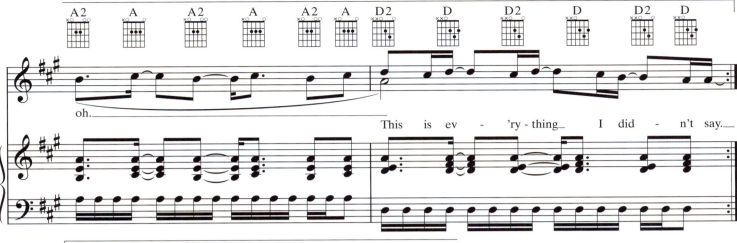

FIREBALL

Words and Music by
ANDREAS SCHULLER, ARMANDO PEREZ,
ERIC FREDERIC, JOSEPH SPARGUR,
ILSEY JUBER, JOHN RYAN and TOM PEYTON

Fireball - 11 - 1

Chorus:

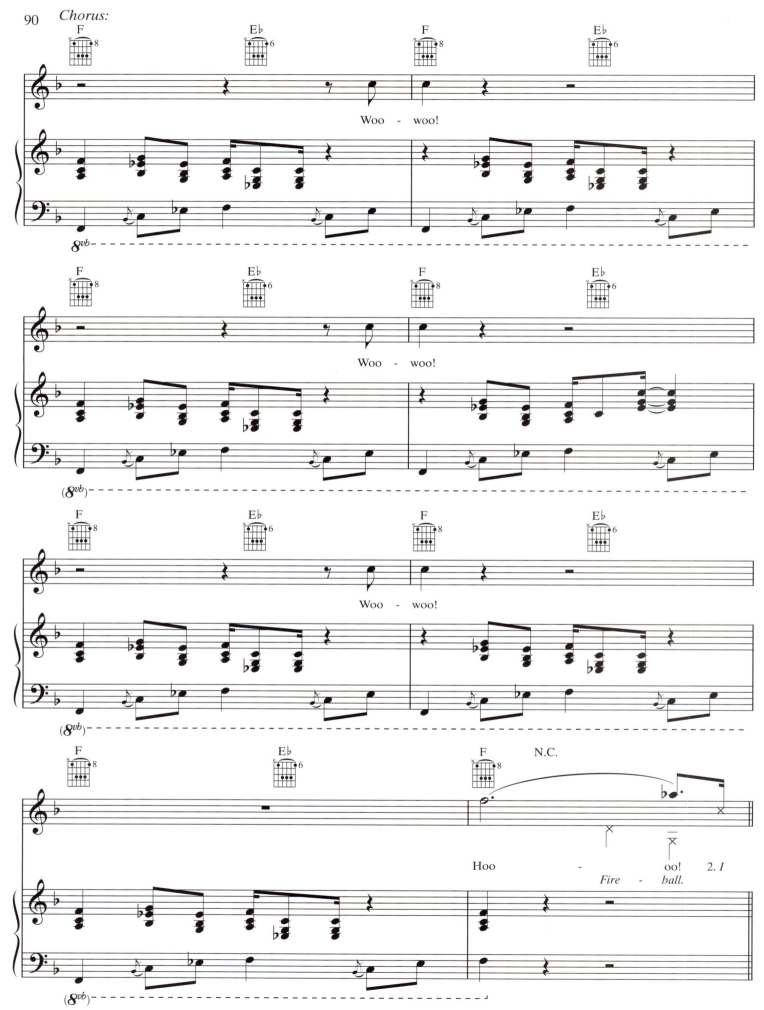

Verses 2 & 3:

3. See additional lyrics

saw, I came,_ I con-quered or should I say I saw, I con-quered, I came?_ They say the

chi - co on fire, he ain't_ no liar,_ while y'all slip-pin' he run-nin' the game._ Now

big bang boog-ie get that kit - ty lit - tle noog-ie in a nice nice lit - tle shade._ I gave

Su - zie a lit - tle pat up on the boo - ty and she turned a-round and said: "walk this way."_ I was born_

Pre-chorus:

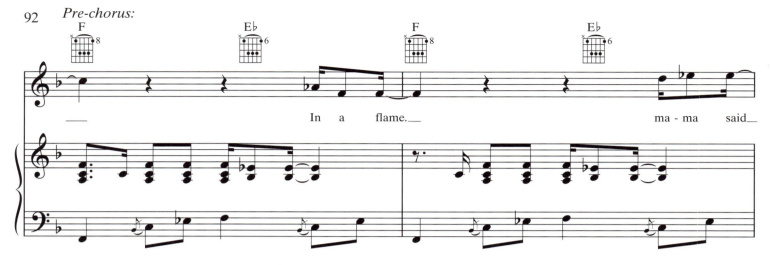

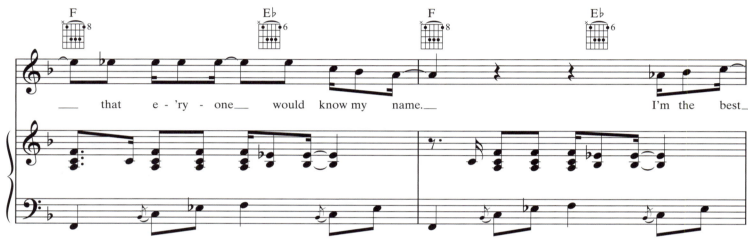

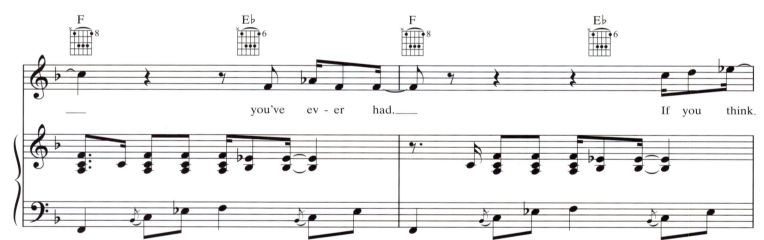

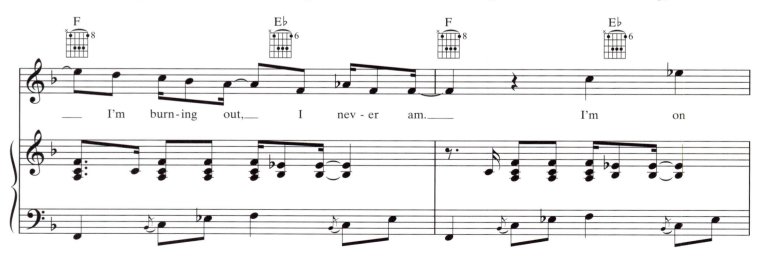

93

Fireball - 11 - 6

Chorus:

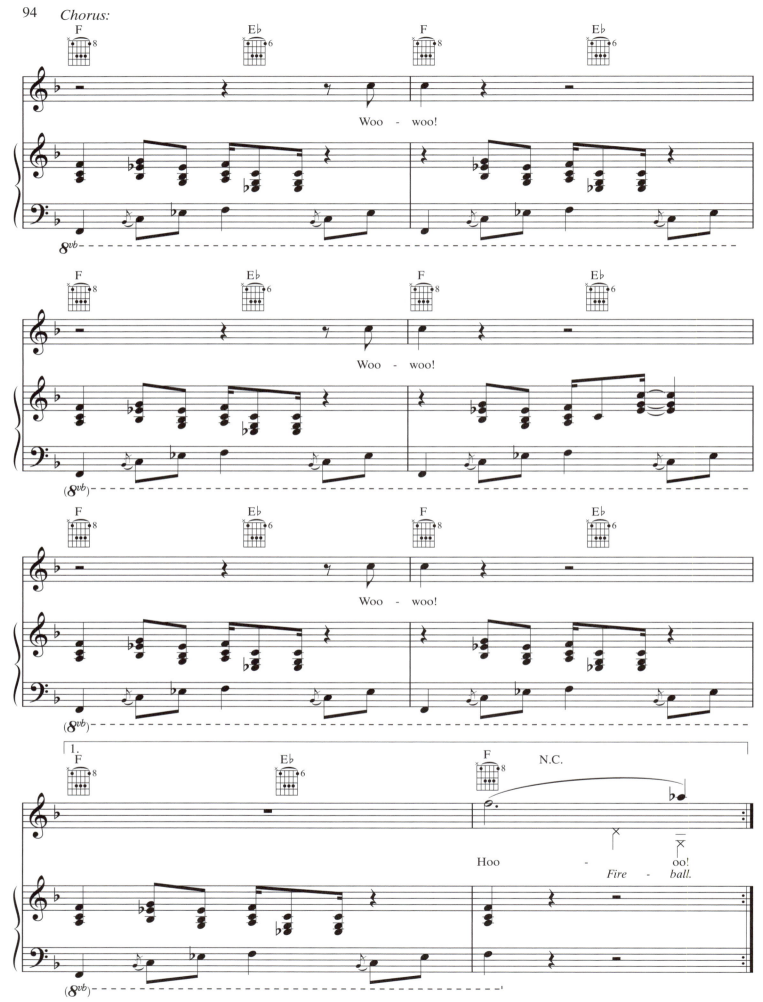

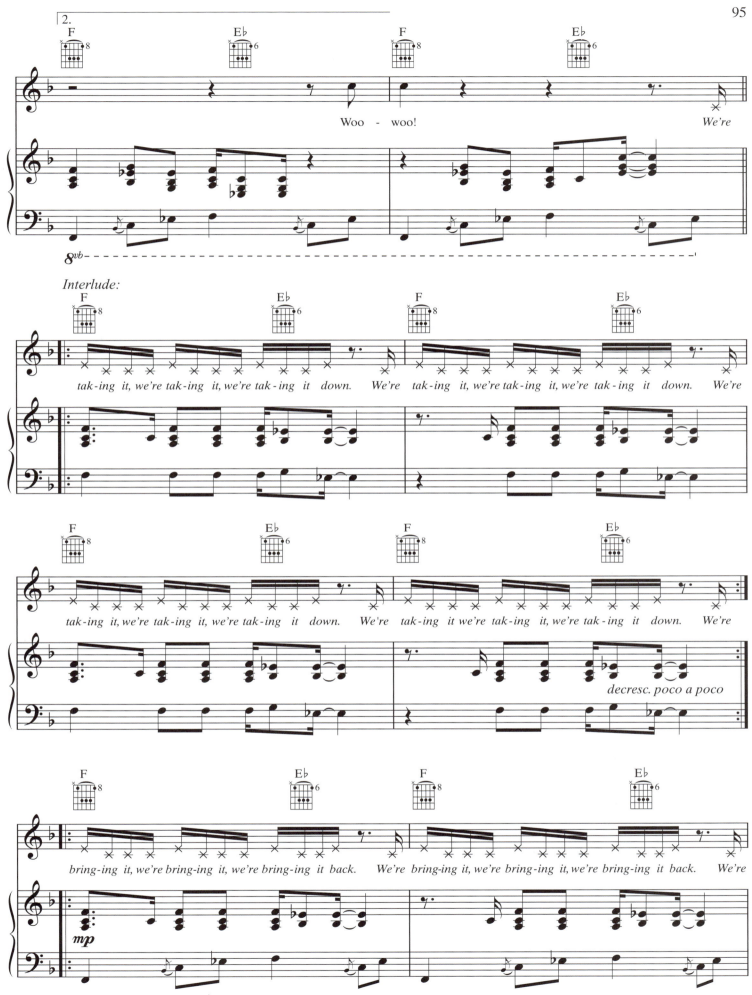

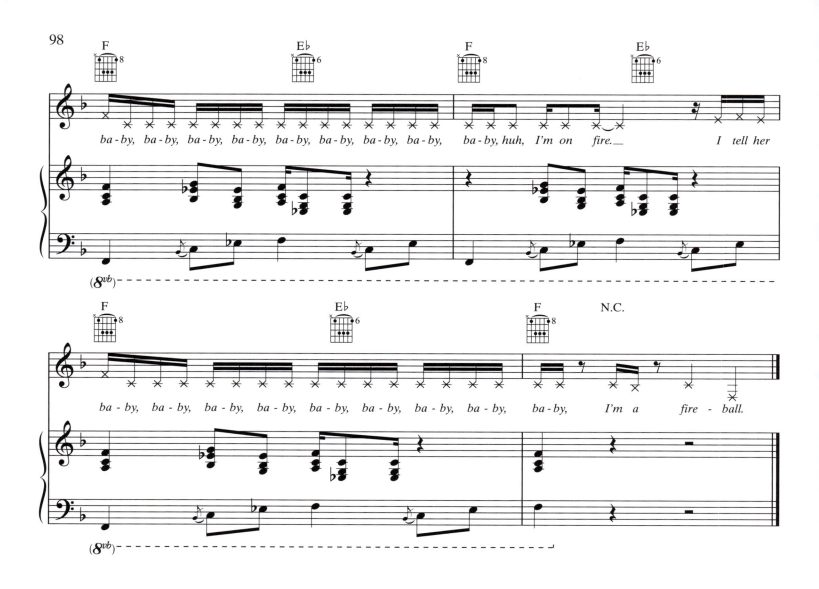

Verse 3:
Sticks and stones may break my bones
But I don't care what y'all say
'Cause as the world turns, y'all boys gonna learn
That this chico right here don't play
That boy's from the bottom, bottom of the map
M.I.A. U.S.A.
I gave Suzie a little pat up on the booty
And she turned around and said,
"Walk this way"
(To Pre-chorus:)

I SEE FIRE

Words and Music by
ED SHEERAN

stand by and_ we__ will_ watch the flames burn au - burn on_____ the moun-tain side._____

Verse 2:

2. And if we should die to - night,_ we should

all die_ to-geth-er._ raise a glass_ of wine_____ for the last___ time. Call-ing

out fath-er,___ oh, pre-pare as__ we___ will__ watch the flames burn au - burn on___ the

moun-tain side.___ Des-o - la - tion comes__up-on the sky._____ Now I see

Chorus:

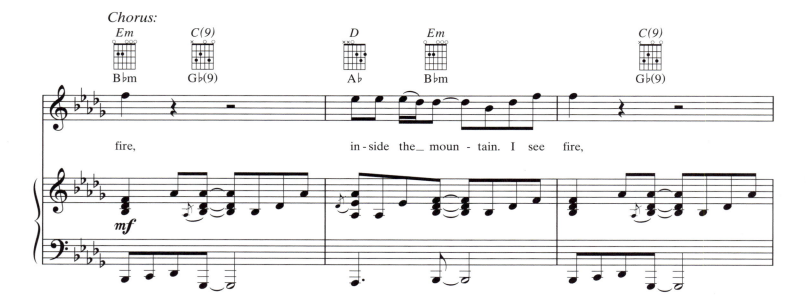

fire, in-side the__ moun - tain. I see fire,

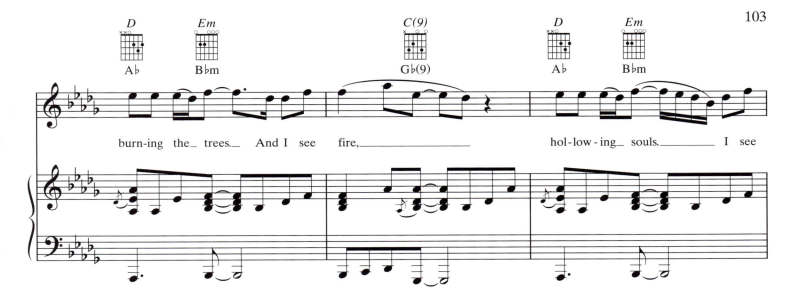

burn-ing the_ trees.__ And I see fire,_____ hol-low-ing_ souls._____ I see

fire,_____ blood in the_ breeze._____ And I hope that you'll_ re - mem - ber me.

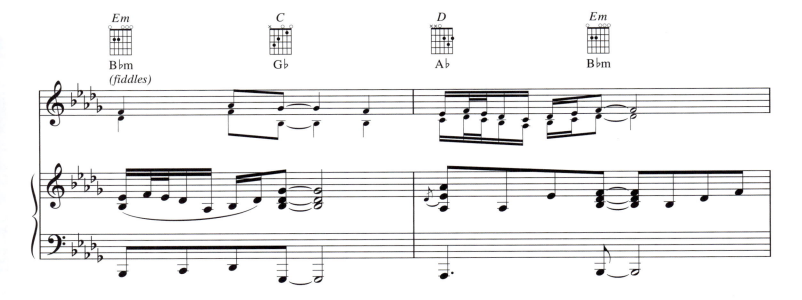

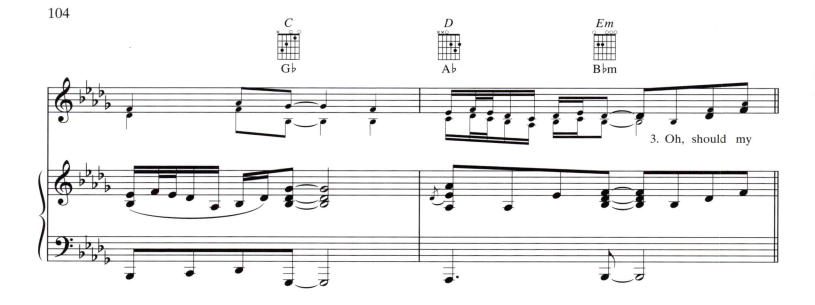

Verse 3:

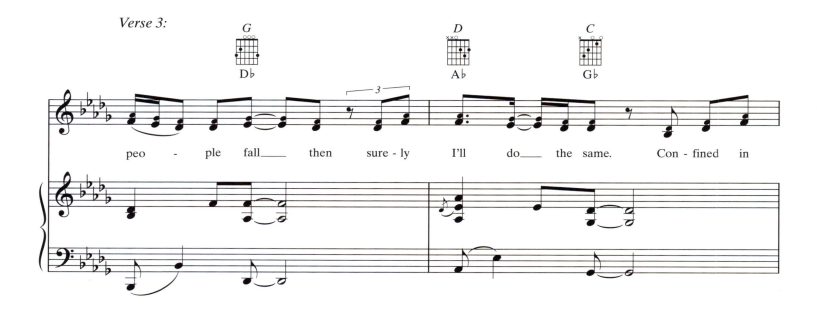

peo - ple fall____ then sure - ly I'll do____ the same. Con - fined in

moun - tain halls,____ we got too close to___ the flame. Call - ing out fath - er,_____ oh,

hold fast and_ we____ will_ watch the flames burn au - burn on_____ the moun-tain side.__ Des-o-

la - tion comes___ up-on the sky._____ Now I see

Chorus:

fire, in-side the_ moun - tain. I see fire,

burn-ing the_ trees._ And I see fire_____ hol-low-ing_ souls._____ I see

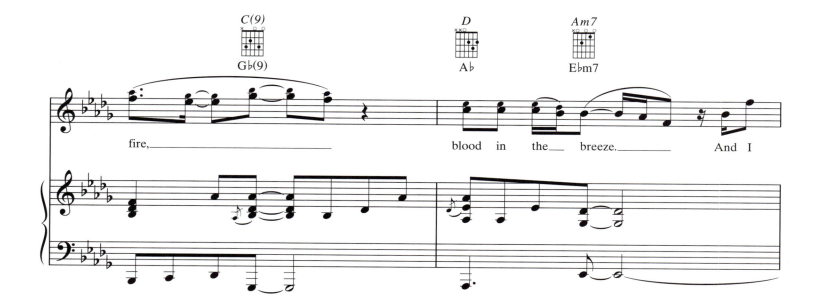

fire,_____ blood in the_ breeze._____ And I

hope that you_ re-mem - ber me._____ And if the__

night is burn - ing I will cov - er my_ eyes._ For if the dark re - turns_ then my

broth-ers will_ die.   And as the sky is fall - ing down,_ it crashed in - to_ this lone-ly town._ And with that

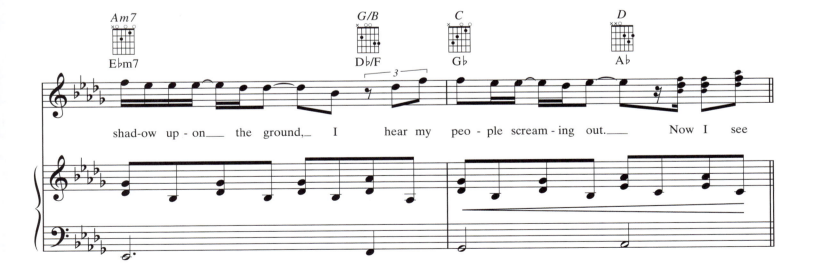

shad-ow up - on_ the ground,_ I hear my peo - ple scream - ing out._ Now I see

Chorus:

fire,   in - side the__ moun - tains. I see fire,

burn-ing the__ trees.__ And I see   fire,_____   hol-low-ing__ souls._____ I see

fire,_____   blood in the__ breeze._____   I see

GODZILLA!
(Main Title Theme)

Composed by
ALEXANDRE DESPLAT

Moderately ♩ = 100

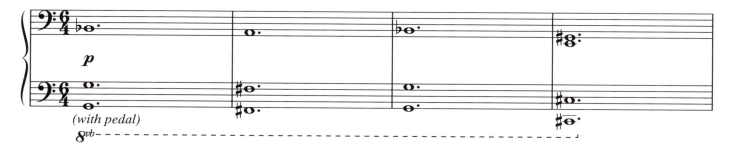

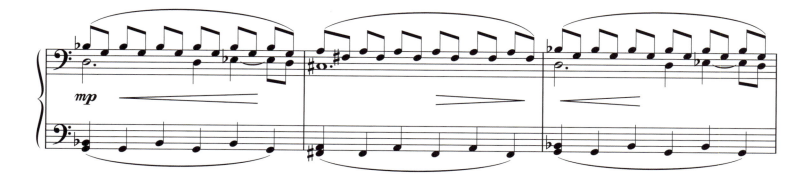

Godzilla! - 4 - 1

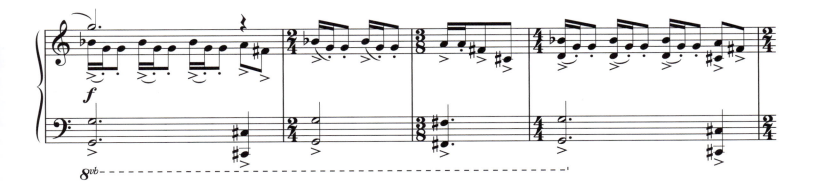

LET IT GO

(from Walt Disney's *Frozen*)

Music and Lyrics by
KRISTEN ANDERSON-LOPEZ
and ROBERT LOPEZ

Moderately, with a half-time feel (♩ = 137)

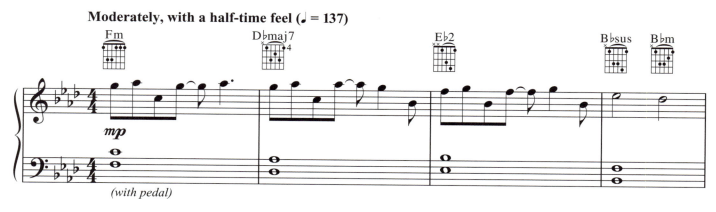

(with pedal)

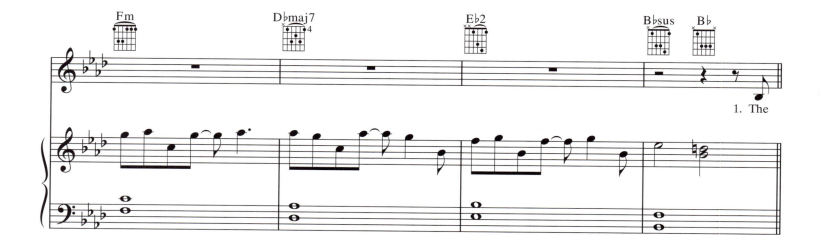

1. The

Verse 1:

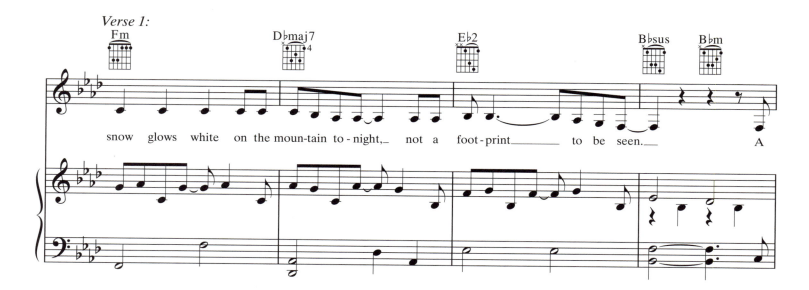

snow glows white on the moun-tain to-night,__ not a foot-print__ to be seen.__ A

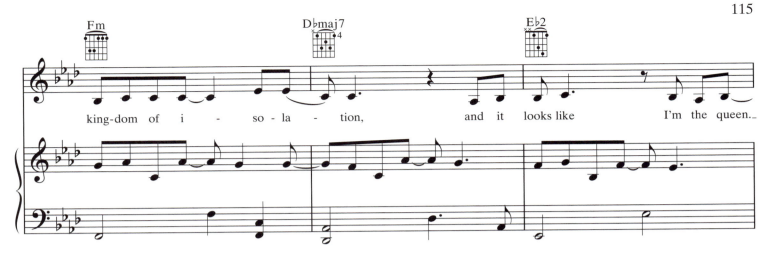

king-dom of i - so - la - tion, and it looks like I'm the queen.

The wind is howl - ing like this

swirl - ing storm in - side. Could-n't keep it in,

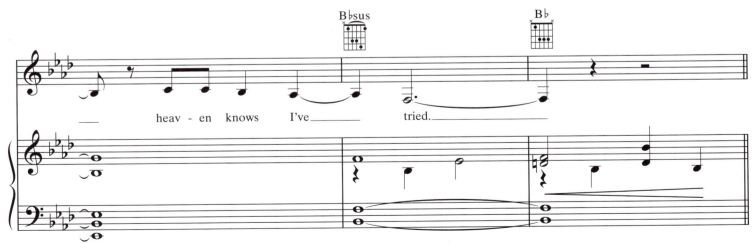

heav - en knows I've tried.

Let It Go - 9 - 2

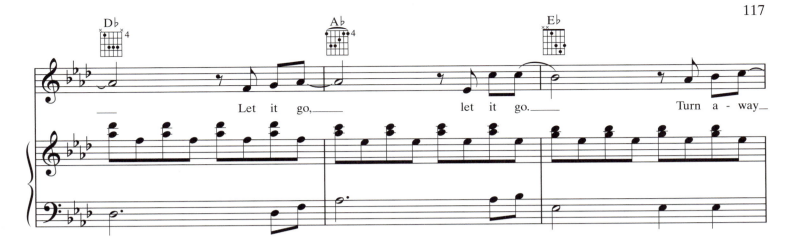

Let it go,____ let it go.____ Turn a - way__

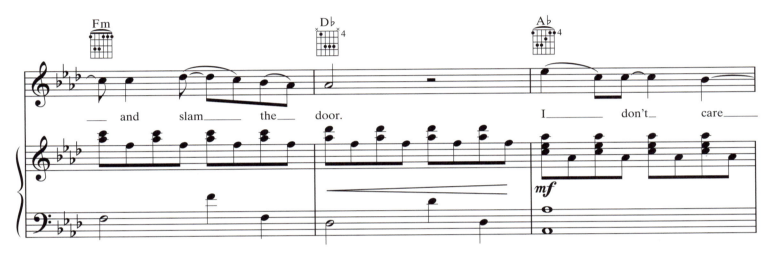

____ and slam____ the__ door. I_____ don't__ care____

____ what they're going to____ say._____ Let the

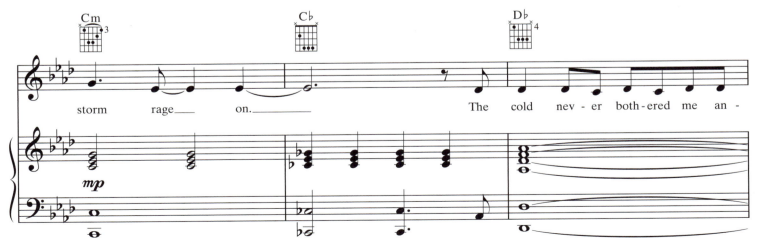

storm rage____ on._____ The cold nev - er both - ered me an -

y - way.

Verse 2:

2. It's fun-ny how some dis - tance makes ev - 'ry-thing__ seem small.__ And the

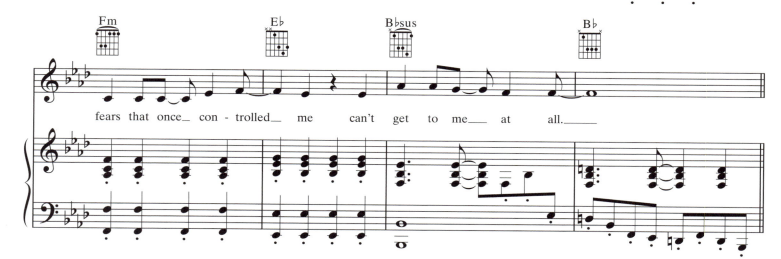

fears that once__ con - trolled__ me can't get to me__ at all.____

It's time__ to see__ what I__ can do__ to test__ the lim - its and__ break

and here I'll____ stay.____ Let the storm rage____ on.____

Bridge:

My pow - er flur-

ries through_ the air____ in - to___ the ground__

My soul__ is spi - ral - ing__ in fro - zen frac - tals all__

Eb5

__ a - round. And one__ thought crys - tal - liz - es like__

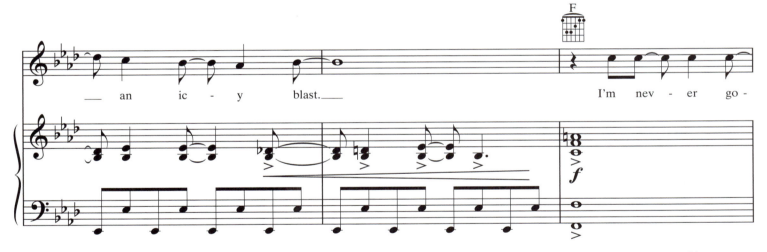

F

__ an ic - y blast.__ I'm nev - er go -

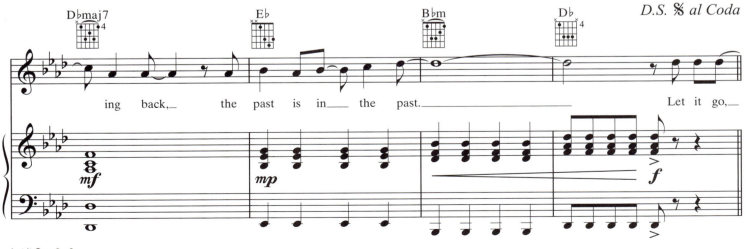

Dbmaj7   Eb   Bbm   Db   *D.S. % al Coda*

ing back,__ the past is in__ the past.__ Let it go,

Let It Go - 9 - 8

122

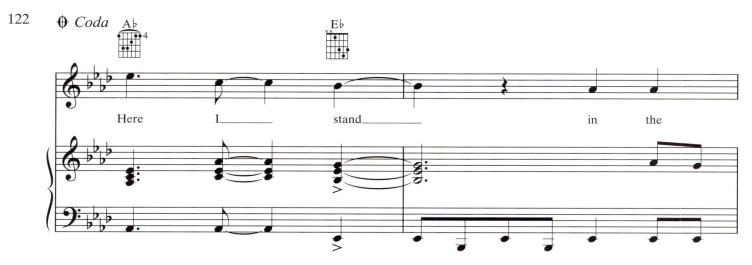

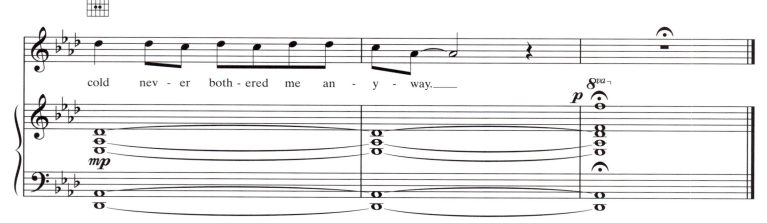

Let It Go - 9 - 9

UP ALL NIGHT

Words and Music by
BRETT BEAVERS, JON PARDI
and BART BUTLER

Verse 1 (sing 1st time only):

1. Yeah, girl, I just had me one hell for-get your flip-flops. We can stop of a work week that's been driv-in' me cra-zy; not e- at a Quick-Stop, get some jerk-y and a 12 pack. No

Verse 2 (sing 2nd time only):

Chorus:

126

get - tin' down, do some up all night._____ 2. Now, don't_

get - tin' down, do some up all night._____

(Guitar solo ad lib....

Bridge:

Come Mon - day I'll___ be back to work-

in' and sav - in', but un - til_____ then...___

Chorus:

_____ Yeah,___ ba - by let's go take a dirt road, kick it back,

find a good song on the ra - di - o 'til we get lost___ in_____ a sun - set

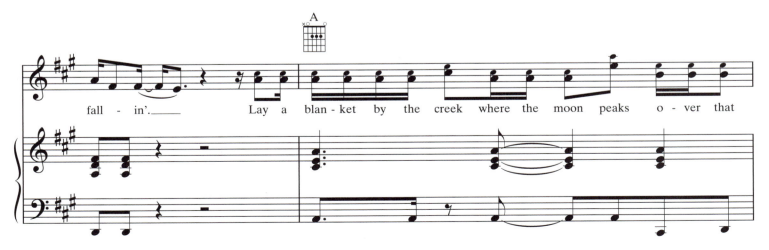

fall - in'._____ Lay a blan - ket by the creek where the moon peaks o - ver that

Na na na na na na____

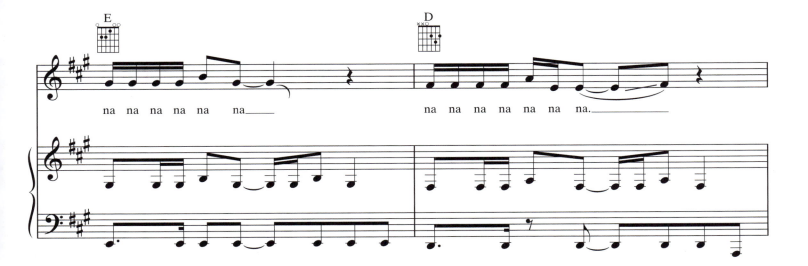

na na na na na na____   na na na na na na na.____

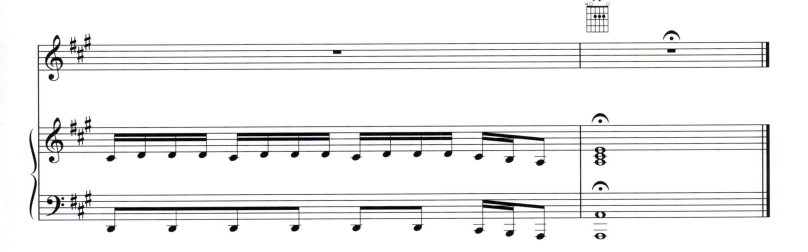

PEOPLE LOVING PEOPLE

Words and Music by
LEE THOMAS MILLER, MICHAEL BUSBEE
and CHRIS WALLIN

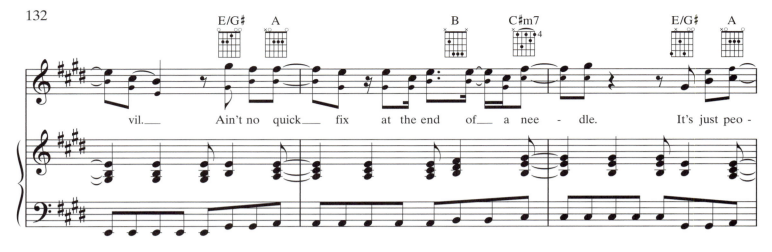

vil.___ Ain't no quick___ fix at the end of___ a nee - dle. It's just peo -

ple a - lov - ing peo - ple.___ Whoa,___ whoa,___

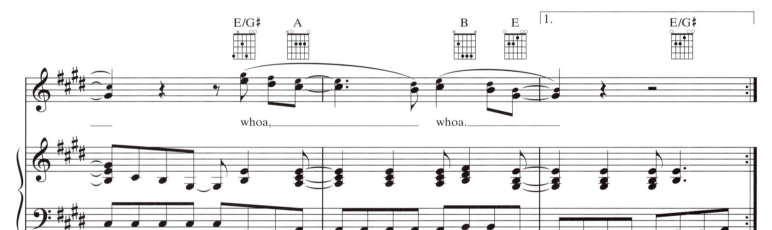

___ whoa,___ whoa.___

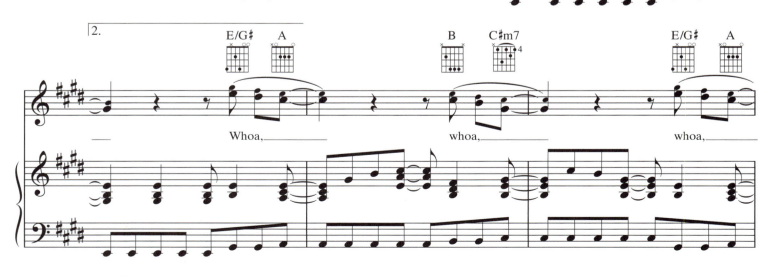

___ Whoa,___ whoa,___ whoa,___

Chorus:

RAINBOW

Words and Music by
ROBERT PLANT, JUSTIN ADAMS,
LIAM TYSON, WILLIAM FULLER
and JOHN BAGGOTT

Moderately bright ♩ = 150

Chorus:

Ooh.

Ooh.

2. I'm reach-ing for the

Ooh.

void shall not wear - y, the fear shall not al - ter. Mm, it's

rain - bow,____ oh, it's rain - bow.____

Oh, can't you see__ the eyes____ are the__ eyes of a lov-

D.S. ℅ al Coda

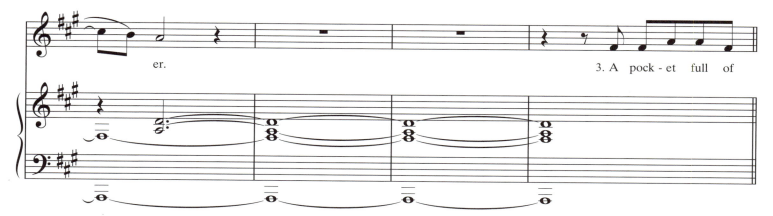

er. 3. A pock - et full of

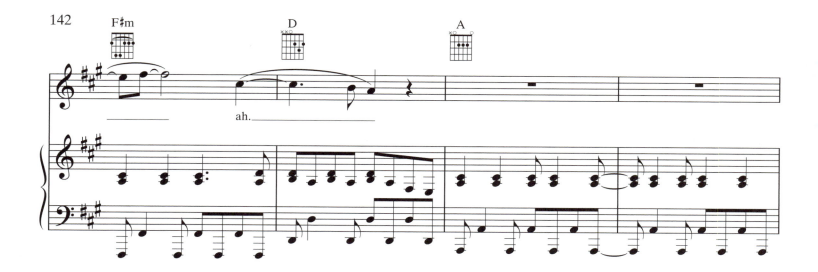

Repeat ad lib. and fade

Rainbow - 8 - 8

SOMETHING IN THE WATER

Words and Music by
CARRIE UNDERWOOD,
CHRIS DeSTEFANO and BRETT JAMES

Moderately bright ♩ = 140

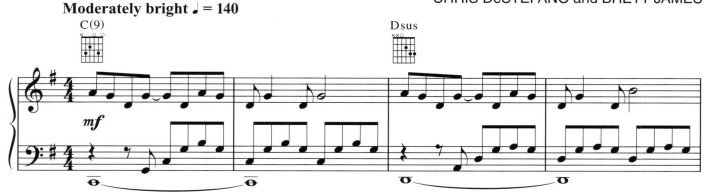

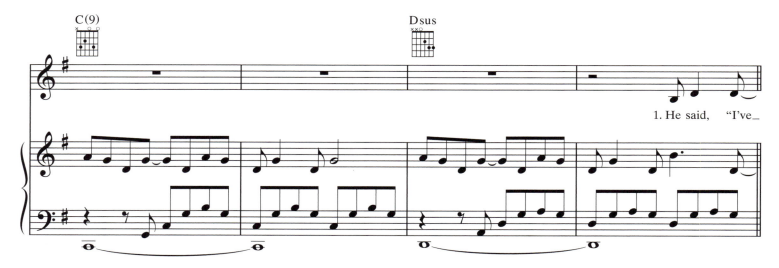

1. He said, "I've

Verse 1: (Sing 1st time only)

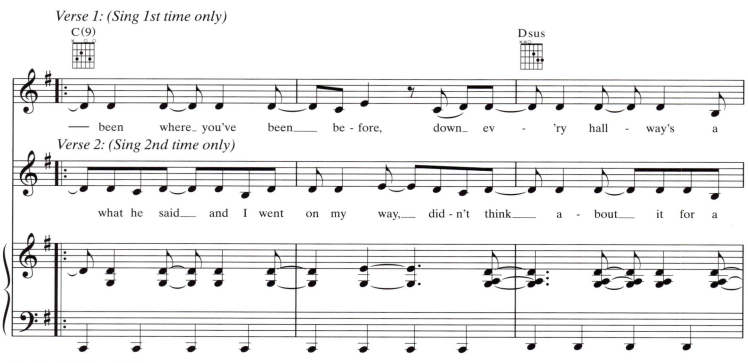

— been where_ you've been_ be - fore, down_ ev - 'ry hall - way's a

Verse 2: (Sing 2nd time only)

what he said_ and I went on my way,_ did - n't think_ a - bout_ it for a

'Just a lit-tle faith,____ it-'ll all____ get bet-ter.' So I fol-
love pour-ing down from____ a - bove,____ got____ washed_

lowed that preach-er man down____ to the riv-er." And now I'm
in the wa - ter,____ washed____ in the blood.___ And now I'm

Chorus:

changed._____

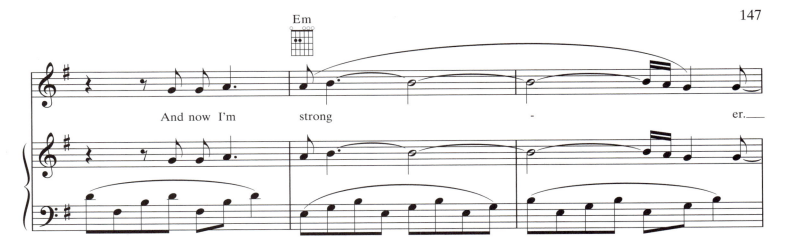

And now I'm strong - er.___

There {must - 've been / must___ be} some-thing in the wa - ter.___

Oh, there {must - 've / must___ be} been some-thing in the

wa - ter._____

ev-'ry day___ giv-ing all___ that I have.___ Trust___ in some - one___ big-

ger than me___ ev - er since___ the day___ that I___ be - lieved.___ I am

Chorus:

changed._____

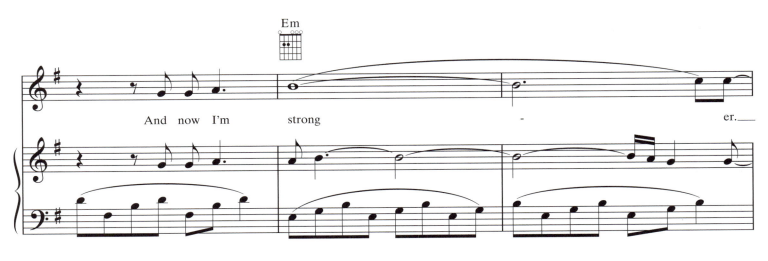

And now I'm strong - er.___

150

Something in the Water - 10 - 7

Oh, there must___ be some-thing in the

the sound that___

wa - ter.___ Oh, there must_

saved a_____ wretch_____

___ be some-thing in the wa - ter.___

___ like_____ me.___

152

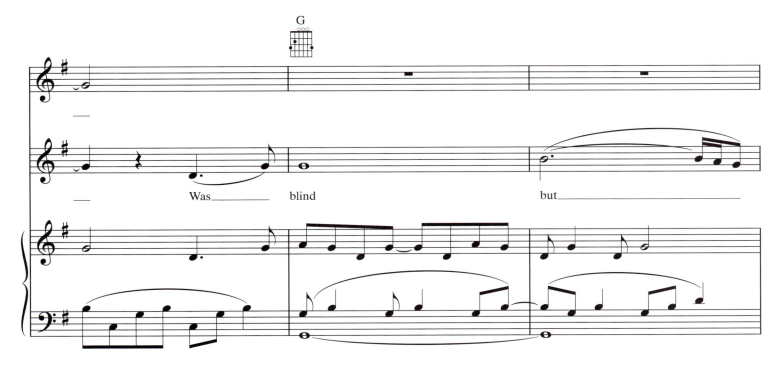

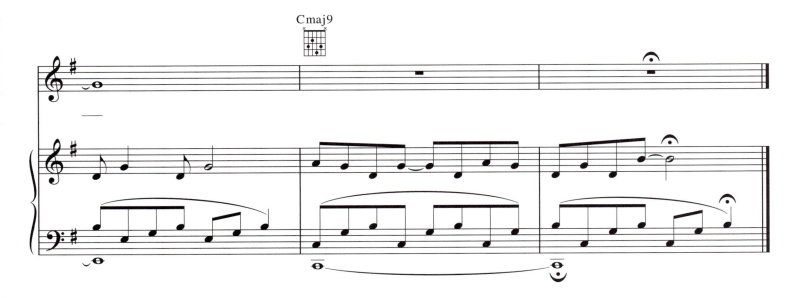

WORDS AS WEAPONS

Words and Music by
SHAUN WELGEMOED, DALE STEWART
and JOHN HUMPHREY

Moderate rock ♩ = 112

*N.C.

All I real-ly want is some-thing beau-ti-ful to say.___ All I real-ly want is some-thing

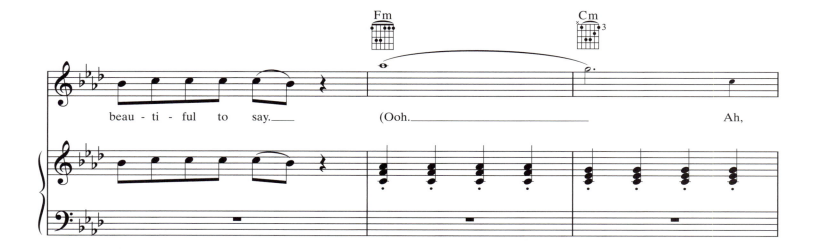

beau-ti-ful to say.___ (Ooh._____ Ah,

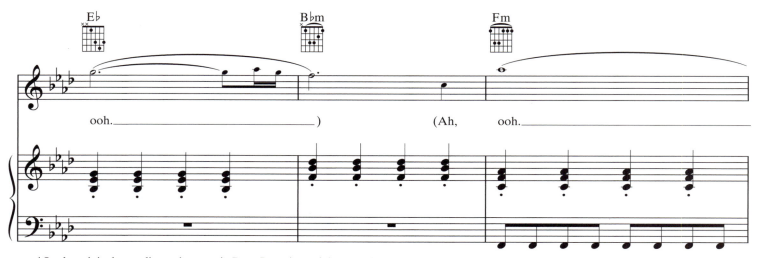

ooh._____) (Ah, ooh.___

*On the original recording guitars are in Drop D, and tuned down 1 whole step.